My First
READ-TOGETHER
Bible

Retold by Mary Batchelor and Penny Boshoff
Illustrated by Clare Fennell

Make
Believe
Ideas

To

....

From

....

Date

....

CONTENTS

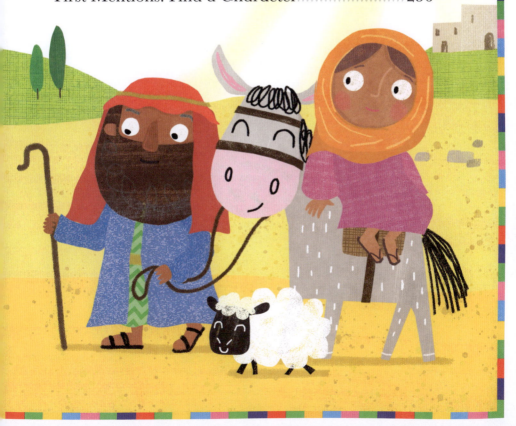

INTRODUCTION

The **Bible** is made up of many stories, but it's also one **great big story!** The big story is about how **God made all of us** and how we have **spoile** his world by doing bad things. But it also shows how **God loves us** becaus he sent **Jesus,** his Son, to fix everything so we can be God's **friends** again

On every page, there are words in **different colors** to help you **understand** the story better. You could even talk about them with your friends and family. Take a closer look at the next two stories.

Find the good things that happen.
Can you see any bad things?

If you see a yellow word, think about why it is important to the story.

NOAH and the **FLOOD**

Nobody on Earth listened to God – except **Noah.**

"**Noah,** there's going to be a flood," said **God.**

"Build a big boat for your **family.** And take two of every kind of animal and bird with you."

Noah did what **God** told him. Then it rained and rained. Water covered the land. But **Noah's** boat floated safely.

18

Genesis 6–7

19

How are people feeling in the story?

Names of characters are in **black** or gray.
The **green** words show **where**
the stories are taking place.

Scan here to hear
the story being read aloud.
You can read along if you like!

RAINBOW in the SKY

Scan to listen.

At last, the rain stopped. When the
land was **dry**, **Noah** opened the door.

Out flew the birds. Off scampered
the animals. And **Noah** said a special
thank-you to God.

"**Noah**," said **God**, "when you see
the **rainbow**, **remember** my promise;
I will **never flood** the whole **Earth** again."

Genesis 8–9

20

21

Look out for the times **God** is mentioned.
Did you know that **God** is
Father, Son, and **Holy Spirit?**

When you see a
rainbow word,
shout it out!

Follow the Scripture
reference to find out
more about the story.

Color Key

Blue – something good happens

Black/gray – characters in the story

Green – places in the story

Navy – God is mentioned

Pink – what people are feeling

Rainbow – an exciting moment

Red – something bad happens

Yellow – important moment in the story

Turn the page to start discovering
the amazing things that God does.

OLD TESTAMENT Stories

MAKING our WORLD

Long ago, when **God** began to **make** everything, the **Earth** was dark and empty.

God said, **"Earth** needs light." And **light appeared.** **God** made the Sun to **shine** by day and the Moon and stars to **light** the night.

God was **pleased** with what he had done.

GOD fills the WORLD

God said, "I will make grass and flowers and trees to cover Earth."

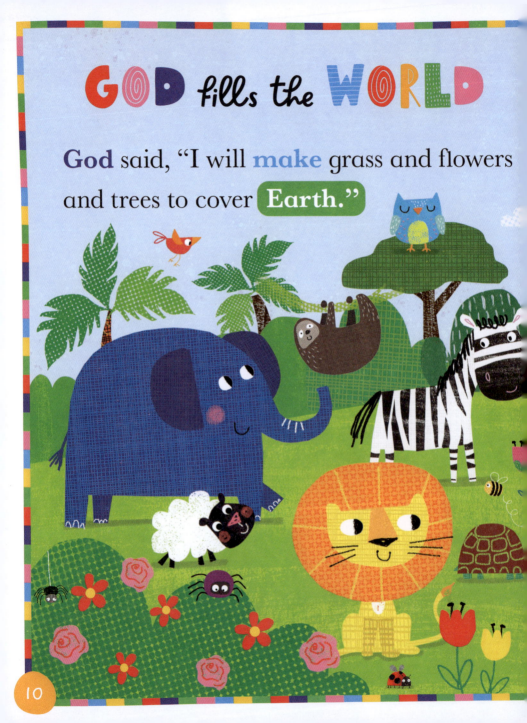

Then he **made** all kinds of **creatures.**

He **made** fish to **swim** in the **rivers** and **seas.** Birds and butterflies to **fill** the **air.** And animals, big and small, to **play** on the **land.**

Genesis 1

11

ADAM and EVE

God said, "Now I will make **people** to take care of the **Earth.**" So he **made** **Adam** and **Eve.**

"**Enjoy** the fruit in my **garden,**" said **God.** Then he pointed to one **tree.** "**Don't eat** fruit from that tree. If you do, you will **die.**"

Adam and **Eve** were very happy in **God's garden.**

Forbidden

The fruit on the **forbidden** tree looked **delicious.** "Why not try it?" the **snake** asked. "But God said we would **die,**" said **Eve.**

"**Don't** listen to **God,**" the **snake** whispered.

Scan to listen.

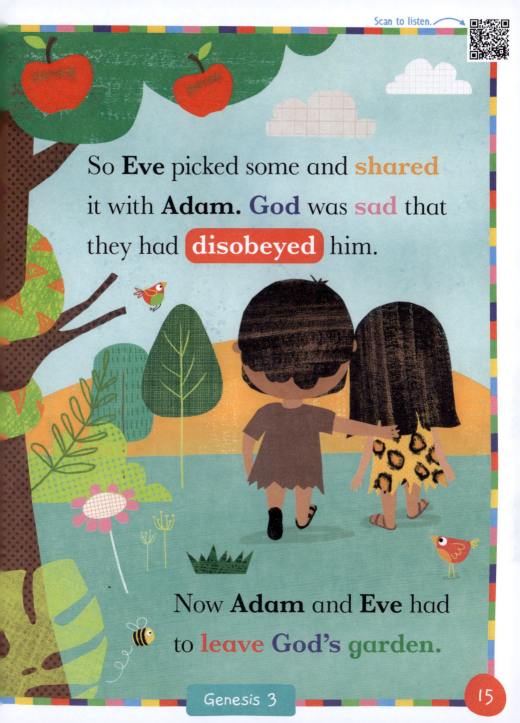

So **Eve** picked some and shared it with **Adam. God** was sad that they had disobeyed him.

Now **Adam** and **Eve** had to leave God's garden.

Genesis 3

CAIN and ABEL

Adam and **Eve** had two sons: **Cain** and **Abel**. **Cain** thought that **God** loved **Abel** more than him. So he hated his brother more and more.

One day when they were out in the **fields, Cain** killed **Abel.**

God was very sad. **Hate** and **murder** were **spoiling** his **Earth. Cain** had to **leave home** and move **far away.**

Genesis 4

NOAH and the FLOOD

Nobody on **Earth** listened to **God** – except **Noah.**

"**Noah,** there's going to be a **flood,**" said **God.**

"**Build** a big boat for your **family.** And take **two** of every kind of animal and bird with you."

Noah did what **God** told him. Then it rained and rained. Water **covered** the **land.** But **Noah's** boat **floated safely.**

19

RAINBOW in the SKY

At last, the rain **stopped.** When the **land** was **dry,** **Noah** opened the door.

Out flew the birds. Off scampered the animals. And **Noah** said a special **thank-you** to God.

"**Noah**," said **God**, "when you see the **rainbow, remember** my promise; I will **never flood** the whole **Earth** again."

Genesis 8–9

21

GOD chooses ABRAHAM

Abraham and **Sarah** longed for a baby. One day **God** said, **"Abraham,** I've chosen you.

"I will give you a new land and a big **family. Everyone** in the whole world will be happy because of you and your **family.**

"So **leave** your **house** and take your tent. We're going on a **journey**."

Three STRANGERS

One hot day **Abraham** saw three tired **strangers**. "Come and **rest** here!" he called.

So they sat in the shade while Abraham brought them food and water. He didn't guess that they were **God's** messengers.

"Next year **Sarah** will have a baby boy," they said.

25

ISAAC

God kept his **promise** and baby **Isaac** was **born.**

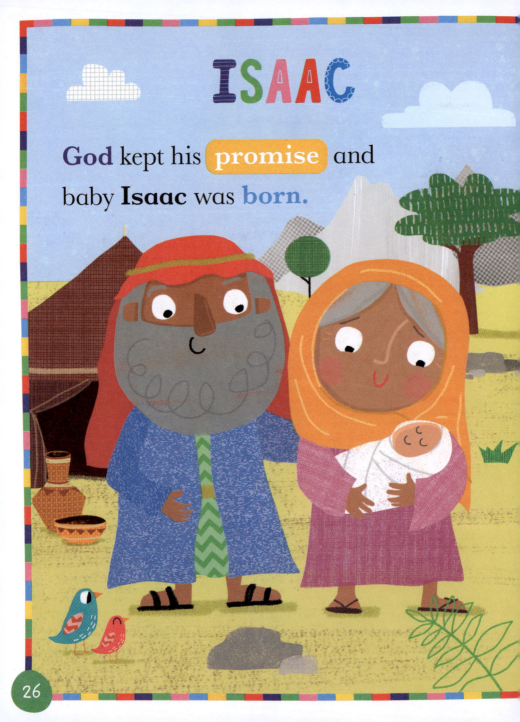

Some years later **God** said, **"Abraham, will you give Isaac back to me?"**

But just as **Abraham** was **getting ready** to give **Isaac** back, **God** called out, **"Abraham,** I know now how much you **love** and **trust** me. I won't take **Isaac** away."

Genesis 22

27

ESAU and JACOB

Isaac **married** Rebekah, and they had twin sons: **Esau** and **Jacob.**

One day **Esau** arrived back from **hunting.**
Jacob was **cooking delicious** food.
"Give me some!" **cried Esau.**
"I'm starving!"

"Only if you **give** me your special place
as oldest son," said **Jacob.**
"All right!" **Esau** agreed.

Genesis 25

29

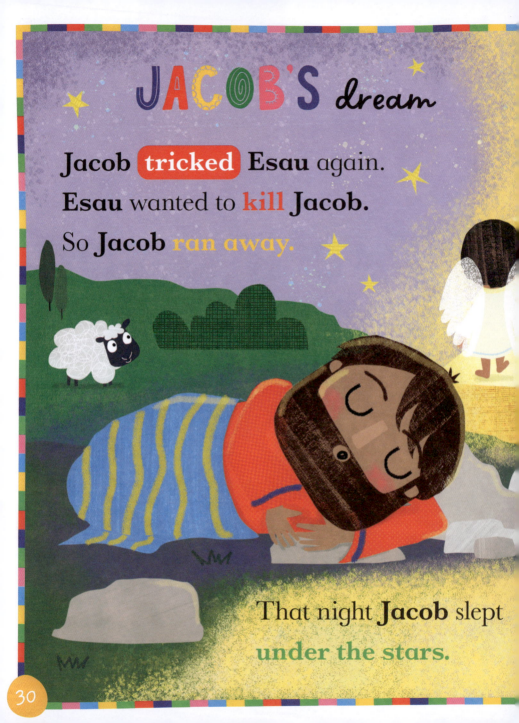

JACOB'S dream

Jacob tricked Esau again.
Esau wanted to kill Jacob.
So Jacob ran away.

That night Jacob slept
under the stars.

30

In his **dream** he saw a staircase. **Angels** were going up and down.

Then **God** said, **"Jacob,** I **promise** to be with you. I'll never leave you. You and your **family** will have the good things I promised to **Abraham."**

Genesis 27–28

31

JOSEPH'S coat

Jacob had lots of children, but he **loved Joseph** the most. He gave **Joseph** a **beautiful coat.** **Joseph's brothers** were **jealous.**

One day **Joseph** went to the **fields** to find his **brothers.**

"Let's **get** him," the **brothers** cried. They **grabbed** **Joseph**, **ripped** off his **special coat,** and **threw** him down an empty **well.**

Genesis 37

JOSEPH goes to EGYPT

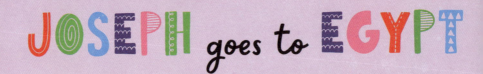

The **brothers** decided to **sell** Joseph to some **men** journeying to **Egypt.**

In **Egypt,** **Joseph** became **Potiphar's** slave.

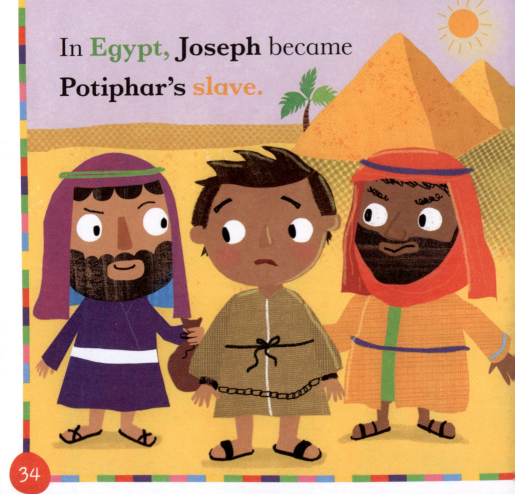

Because **Joseph** worked so hard, **Potiphar** put him in charge of everything he had.

But **Potiphar's wife** told lies about **Joseph,** so he was sent to prison. Even there, **God** was still with him.

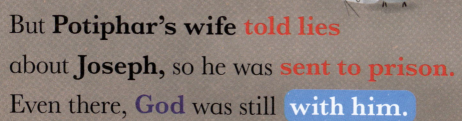

Genesis 37, 39

35

JOSEPH saves EGYPT

The **king** of **Egypt** had worrying dreams. **"Fetch** Joseph," a **servant** said. "He understands dreams."

The **king** told **Joseph** his dream. **"God** says seven **good** harvests are coming, followed by seven **bad** ones," **Joseph explained.** "Save food now to **feed** your **people** in the bad years."

36

The **king** was pleased. "**Joseph,** you must help me lead **Egypt.**"

BROTHERS reunited

Now **Joseph's brothers** had to travel to **Egypt** to buy corn. They **did not know** that the man in charge was **Joseph.** Joseph **pretended** to be **angry.**

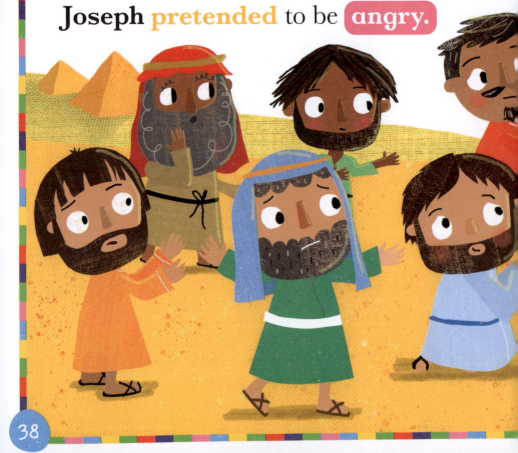

Then he said, "Don't be **frightened.**
It's me, **Joseph!** I will take care of you.
God brought me here to **save everyone!**
Come and **live** in **Egypt.**"

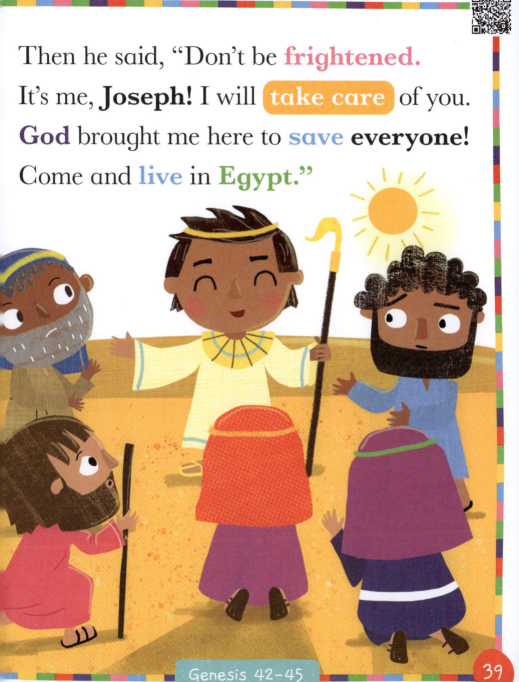

Genesis 42–45

39

MOSES

God gave **Jacob** the name "Israel." **Israel's people** stayed in **Egypt.** But years later a **cruel king** made them his **slaves.** "Kill all their baby **boys,**" he ordered.

But one **mother** hid her **baby** in a floating basket among the **river reeds.** "What's in that basket?" asked the **princess.** Her **servant** opened the lid. "What a **beautiful baby!**" the **princess** exclaimed. "I shall keep him and name him **Moses.**"

Exodus 1-2

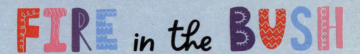

FIRE in the BUSH

When **Moses** grew up, he longed to
save his **people**. The **king** was furious
so **Moses** ran far away.

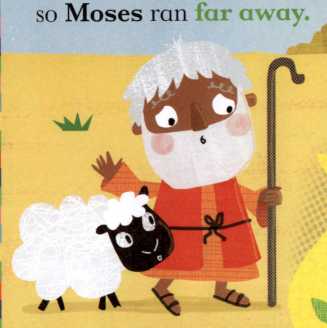

One day **Moses** saw
a bush on fire.
"That's strange!" he thought.

Suddenly **God** spoke from the **bush.** **"Moses,** go back to Egypt and **rescue** your **unhappy people."**

"I **can't!"** **Moses** exclaimed. "Yes, you can," **God** said, "because I will be with you."

Exodus 3

43

MOSES warns the KING

Moses set off for Egypt.
"God says you must let his
people go," he told the king.

"NO!" the king replied.
"I don't know or care
about your God.
I won't let them go.
Make the Israelites
work harder!"

"Obey **God** or **bad things** will happen," **Moses** warned.

"I **won't!**" the **king** replied.

CHAOS in EGYPT

Everything **happened** as **Moses** had **warned.** First frogs ran **everywhere,** then flies came, then there were storms. But still the **king** would **not let** the **Israelites** go.

"God will **rescue** his **people,"** **Moses** said, "but because of you, **Egypt** will be **sad." "Go away!"** the **king** shouted.

"Tomorrow **God** will **rescue** us," **Moses** told the **Israelites.** "Cook a **special meal** to **thank** him."

The WAVES roll back

The next day the **Israelites** left **Egypt** and camped by the Red Sea. But the **Egyptian army** chased them!

God said, **"Moses, stretch** your stick over the sea. Tell the **people** to go forward."

Moses obeyed **God.** The waters rolled back, and the **Israelites** crossed on **dry ground.** "Hooray!" they shouted on the **other side. "God** has rescued us!"

49

GOD sends FOOD

"**God** is **leading** us to the **country** he **promised** us," **Moses** told the **Israelite** as they walked through the **desert.**

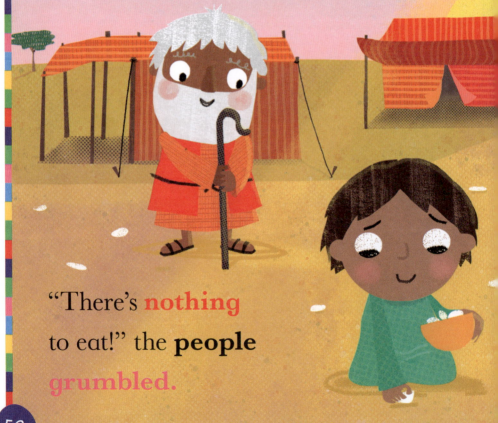

"There's **nothing** to eat!" the **people** grumbled.

"I will feed you every day,"
God promised.
The next morning the ground
was covered with small white flakes.
They tasted good, like honey biscuits.

GOD gives WATER

The **people** kept grumbling. "We're thirsty, **Moses**," they moaned. "Give us water!"

Moses told **God** and **God** said, "**Go** to the special rock that I will show you, and hit it with your stick."

Moses did as **God** told him and cool, refreshing water **gushed** from the **rock.** There was **plenty** for **everyone.**

Exodus 17

53

RULES for the PEOPLE

God said to **Moses,** "These rules will **help** my **people** every day: **Put me first** and love me best. Don't **worship** anyone but me. Don't use my name **carelessly. Keep** one day each week as a **resting day** with me.

"**Obey** your father and mother. Don't **hurt** others. Keep **love** between a husband and wife **special.** Don't **take** what isn't yours. Don't **tell lies** about other people. Don't be **jealous** of other people and **want** what they have."

Scan to listen.

Reaching CANAAN

When they reached the land God had promised them, **Moses** sent twelve **spie**
to look around.

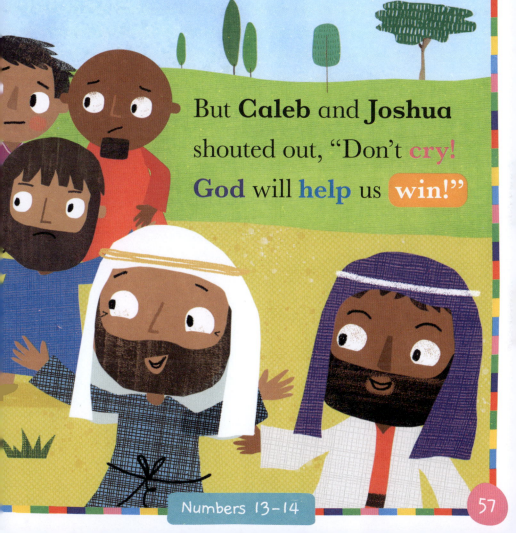

"It's a **wonderful** country," the **spies** said, "but we'll **never** win it! The people there are **huge** and **strong!**"

But **Caleb** and **Joshua** shouted out, "Don't **cry! God** will **help** us **win!**"

Brave RAHAB

When **Moses** died, **God** made **Joshua** the leader. **Joshua** sent two **spies** to **Jericho.**

The **king** sent **soldiers** to seize them, but **Rahab** hid them. Finally the **soldiers** left.

Rahab said to the **spies,** "When **God** gives you **Jericho**, please be kind to me." "We will!" they **promised.**

The walls FALL DOWN

Joshua did **everything** **God** told him.

So for **six days** **Joshua** and the **soldiers** and **priests** marched once around **Jericho.** On the seventh day they **marched** around it **seven times, blowing** their trumpets.

Then **everyone** shouted. At once the walls of the **city** fell. CRASH! But **Rahab** was **not hurt.**

GIDEON

The **Israelites** soon forgot **God.**
But **God** did **not forget** them. When
enemies attacked **Israel, God** said to
Gideon, "Rescue my **people.**
I'll **show** you how!"

That night **Gideon** and his **soldiers** crept to the **enemy camp** with **trumpets** and **jars** with **torches** inside.

At **Gideon's** signal, every **soldier** smashed his jar, **blew** his trumpet, and shouted, "For **God** and for **Gideon!**" And **Israel's enemies** ran away!

Judges 6–7

SAMSON'S riddle

More **enemies** attacked Israel. This time **God** chose strong **Samson** to fight them.

Samson told his **enemies** this riddle: "Out of the eater came something to eat. Out of the strong came something sweet."

Scan to listen.

His enemies, the **Philistines,** were **puzzled.** Then they *discovered* that **Samson** had *found* a bee's nest in a lion's dead body and had eaten the *delicious honey.*

Judges 13–14

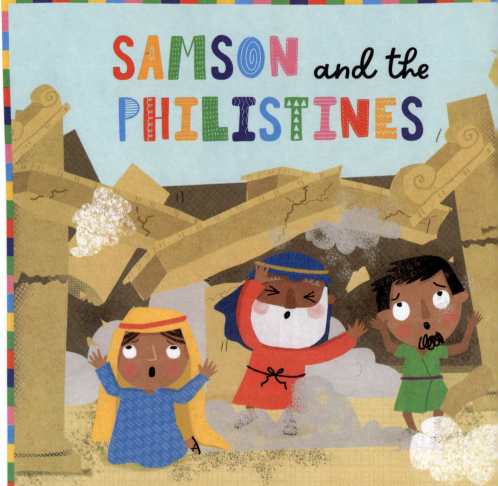

SAMSON and the PHILISTINES

Finally the **Philistines** caught Samso
They **blinded** him and brought him to
their **temple.** "Our god **Dagon** is the
greatest!" they shouted.

"**God,** please **help** me to **beat** the **Philistines,**" Samson prayed.

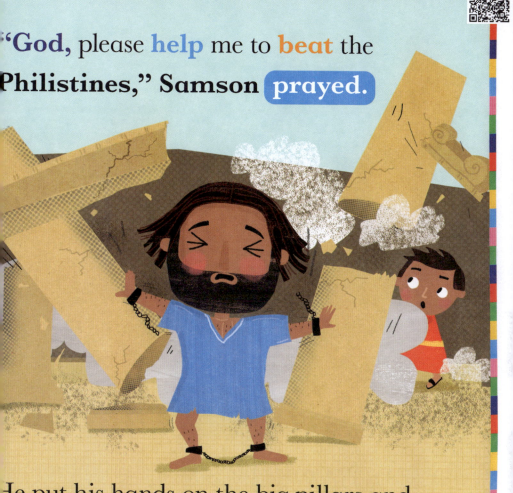

He put his hands on the big pillars and pushed and **pushed.** Crack. **CRASH!** The **temple** fell down and killed **everyone.** Samson was remembered as a great **hero.**

Judges 16

67

NAOMI and RUTH

Naomi's family lived in Bethlehem. But when the **food ran out,** they moved to faraway **Moab.**

Poor **Naomi!** Her **husband** and **sons** died. But their Moabite wives, **Orpah** and **Ruth,** looked after her.

"I'm going back to **Bethlehem,**" **Naomi** said. "Goodbye," said **Orpah,** hugging **Naomi.** But **Ruth** said, "I'm coming with you. I'll stay with you always. I love you, and your **God** will be my **God.**"

Bethlehem

A HAPPY ending

Naomi and **Ruth** arrived in **Bethlehem**
They were so poor that **Ruth**
picked up leftover grain from the
fields to make bread.

"Who's that **stranger?**"
asked the farmer **Boaz.**

"That's **Ruth.** She takes good care of **Naomi,**" the **farmworkers** replied. "Then drop extra grain for **Ruth,**" **Boaz** said kindly. **Boaz** decided to marry **Ruth.**

They soon had a little boy. Now **Naomi** was very happy.

GOD answers a PRAYER

Hannah longed for a baby! One day she visited **God's house** with her **husband. Hannah** felt so sad.

"Please, **God,**" she cried, "**send** me a baby. I promise I'll give him back to you." **Eli** the priest heard her.

"May **God** answer your prayer!" he said. And **God** did! **Hannah** called her baby Samuel.

1 Samuel 1

GOD calls SAMUEL

Hannah kept her promise. She took **Samuel** to live with **Eli** the priest at **God's house.**

One night **Samuel** heard a **voice:** **"Samuel!"** He ran to **Eli.** "I didn't call," **Eli** said. "Go back to bed."

Three times Samuel heard the **voice** and **three times** he ran to **Eli.**

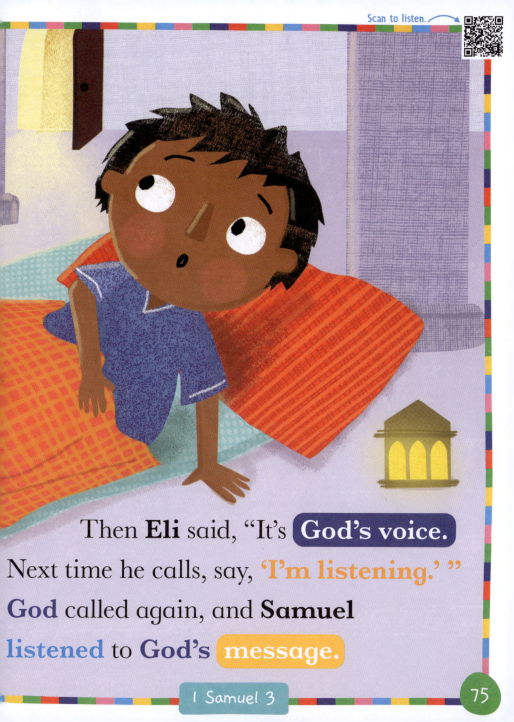

Scan to listen.

Then **Eli** said, "It's **God's voice.**
Next time he calls, say, **'I'm listening.'** "
God called again, and **Samuel**
listened to **God's message.**

1 Samuel 3

75

KING of ISRAEL

Samuel gave God's messages to the **Israelites.** But they wanted a king instead. "I will choose their king," **God** told **Samuel.**

One day a young man called Saul arrived. "My **father's** donkeys **ran away,**" he told **Samuel.** "I can't find them anywhere. Can you help me?"

"Don't **worry,** your donkeys have been **found,**" **Samuel** said. **"God** has chosen you to be **king** of **Israel!"**

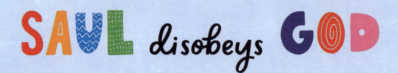

SAUL disobeys GOD

One day the **Israelites** were getting ready for **battle.** "**Wait** for me to **pray** before you fight," **Samuel** told **King Saul.**

King Saul waited and waited. Finally he **decided** to say the prayers **himself.** Just then **Samuel** came back.

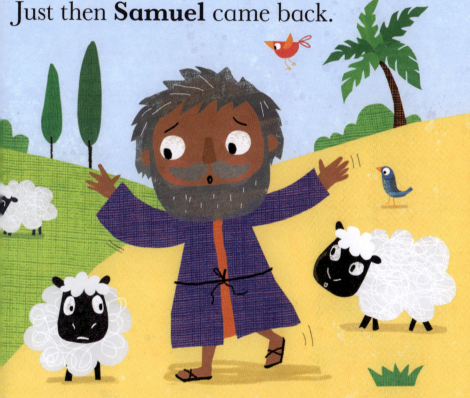

"Why didn't you **wait?**" **Samuel** asked **sadly.** "Because you **won't obey** God, he is going to **choose** another king."

A NEW KING

"Go and see **Jesse**," God told **Samuel.**
"I have chosen one of his **sons** to be
king." **Jesse's** oldest **son** was handsome

"He looks like a king!" thought Samuel.
But **God** whispered, "No! Not this one."

Samuel saw six more **sons.**

But each time **God** said, **"No!"**

"Have you another **son?"** **Samuel** asked.

"Only **young** **David,"** **Jesse** replied.

"He's looking after my sheep."

When **David** arrived,

God told **Samuel,**

"He is the one!

My chosen king!"

1 Samuel 16

81

DAVID and GOLIATH

David's brothers were in **Saul's** army. **David** was visiting them when the huge Philistine soldier **Goliath** bellowed, **"Israelites,** choose a man to fight me!" The **Israelites** were terrified.

"I'll fight him!" said **David,** taking just his shepherd's sling and five stones. "I'll feed you to the birds!" cried **Goliath.** "I fight with **God's** strength!" **David** shouted. He aimed.

The stone from his sling hit **Goliath's** skull… crack! **Goliath** crashed to the ground.

1 Samuel 17

DAVID and JONATHAN

Saul **invited** David to live in his palace. Whenever Saul was **miserable,** David would **sing** and **play his harp** to **cheer** him up.

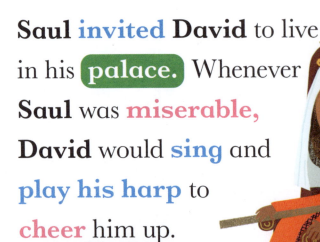

David and Jonathan, Saul's son, became great friends. But Saul grew jealous of David.

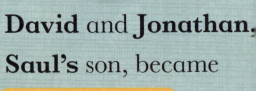

Scan to listen.

One day **Saul** **hurled** his spear at **David.**
David dodged it just in time!

"Go," said **Jonathan,** "or my **father**
will **kill** you!"

The two **friends** hugged each other
and sadly said, "Goodbye."

1 Samuel 16, 18–20

85

SAUL chases DAVID

When **Saul** discovered **David** had gone, he chased him. One night **David** and his nephew **Abishai** crept up on **Saul** and his **soldiers** as they slept. "Kill **Saul** now!" **Abishai** whispered.

"Never!" **David** replied. "**God** would **not want** that. We'll take **Saul's** spear and water jug instead!"

When **Saul** discovered that **David** had taken his spear and jug but had not hurt him, he promised to stop chasing **David.**

1 Samuel 26

87

DAVID becomes KING

One day **Saul** and **Jonathan** died in battle, and **David** became king.

"**Jonathan** is dead," **David** said sadly. "I must look after his **family**."

"Then take care of his son **Mephibosheth**," a **servant** said. "He can't walk."

So **David** **invited** **Jonathan's** son to the **palace.** "**Welcome,** **Mephibosheth,**" he said.

"Come and **live** **here** and **have** **dinner** with me every day."

2 Samuel 9

89

Wise SOLOMON

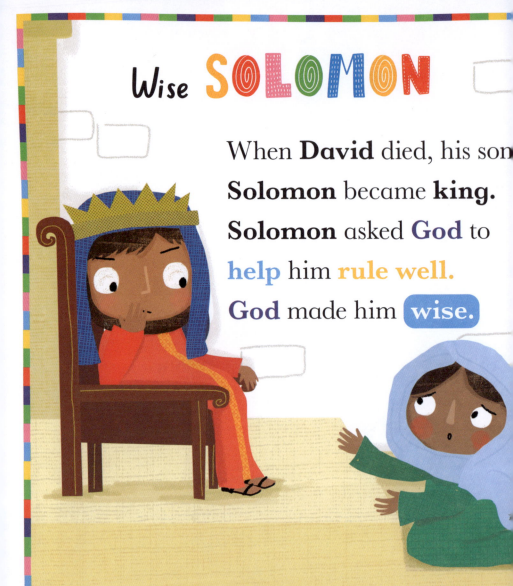

When **David** died, his son **Solomon** became **king**. **Solomon** asked **God** to **help** him **rule well**. **God** made him **wise.**

One day two **mothers** arrived with a **ba**

"He's **my baby!**" the first **woman** cried.

Scan to listen.

"No! He's **mine**," the **other** shouted.

"**Cut** the **baby** in two," ordered

Solomon, "and give each **mother** half!"

"No!" cried the first **woman.**

"**Don't hurt him!**

Let **her** have him!"

"**Take** the **baby**," **Solomon** told the first **woman**, "for you are the **real** mother."

1 Kings 3

91

A TEMPLE for GOD

God made **Solomon** rich as well as **wise. Solomon** began to build a **splendid home** for **God** – the temple.

Thousands of **builders** got **busy** with fine wood and huge stones. Inside, in **God's special room,** even the floor was paved with gold!

Finally it was finished. **Everyone** celebrated. **God** promised to listen to his **people** when they prayed to him there.

Scan to listen.

93

ELIJAH and the BAD KING

Some **kings** of Israel were **bad.** **King Ahab** and his wicked queen, **Jezebel,** prayed to **false gods** and **killed** many of **God's** friends.

94

Scan to listen.

One day **God's** friend **Elijah** brought **Ahab** a message. "I serve the true **God.** There will be no rain until I say so!"

What **Elijah** said came true. Plants and animals began to die. **Everyone** was hungry. But **God** looked after **Elijah.**

1 Kings 16–17

95

The REAL GOD

"Bring the **servants** of the **false god
Baal** to Mount Carmel," **Elijah** told
Ahab. "We'll prove who's the real **God."**
Elijah told **Baal's followers,** "Build a
fire with wood. Now ask **Baal** to
light it." They prayed and prayed
but **nothing happened!**
Elijah poured water over his wood.
Then he **prayed:** "Please, God,
send fire!" At once fire **streaked** down
and set **Elijah's** wood **alight.**
"Our **God** is the real **God!"** shouted
the **Israelites.**

97

ELIJAH and ELISHA

Jezebel was furious.
She wanted to **kill** Elijah.
But **God** kept him safe.

"Find **Elisha**," **God** told
Elijah. "He'll help you.
He will be my
messenger too."

One day **Elijah** and **Elisha** were walkin
together when they heard a **rushing noi**
Suddenly a chariot of fire, drawn by
fiery horses, swooped down between them

Scan to listen.

A **great wind** whirled **Elijah** off his feet. He was **lifted** up, up, and away until **Elisha** could see him no more.

ONE BOTTLE of oil

A **widow** came to **Elisha.** "Help me!" she **sobbed.** "They're **taking** my **sons** away because I **owe** money." "What have you got at **home?**" **Elisha** asked. "One small **bottle of oil,**" she said.

"Borrow lots more bottles and **fill them** with your oil," **Elisha** said. The **boys** fetched bottles, and their **mother** poured and poured...

The oil didn't run out until every borrowed bottle was full!
"Now sell the oil to pay your debt," said kind **Elisha**.

2 Kings 4

101

NAAMAN is healed

Naaman, chief of the **Syrian army,** had a terrible **skin disease.** His young Israelite **servant girl** said, "Go to **Elisha, God's** messenger in **Israel.** He will **make you better.**"

"**Wash** seven times in the **river Jordan,**" **Elisha** told **Naaman.** "I can wash in **cleaner rivers** back **home!**" **Naaman** **shouted** angrily.

"Please **do** as **Elisha** says!" his **soldiers** **pleaded.** So **Naaman** **dipped** in the **river** seven times, and his skin was **smooth** again!

"Your **God** is the **real** **God!**" **Naaman** told **Elisha.**

KING JOASH

After **King Ahaziah** died, his mother **Athaliah** killed all the royal children to become queen!

But baby **Joash** was rescued by his aunt. She hid him in **God's temple.**

When **Joash** was seven, the priest **Jehoiada** invited the **people** to the **temple.** He led **Joash** out, placed a crown on his head, and gave him a copy of **God's** Law. **Everyone** cheered, "Long live **King Joash!**"

Athaliah was furious. Now **Joash** was **God's king.**

2 Kings 11–12

JONAH and the BIG FISH

God told **Jonah,** "**Go** to the **people** of **Nineveh. Tell** them to stop being **wicked** **Jonah didn't want** to go. He **ran away** and went to **sea.**

But **God** sent a strong wind to **whip up** the waves. "We're going to **sink!**" cried the terrified sailors.

"It's **my fault!**" **Jonah** said. "I **ran away** from **God.** Throw me in the **sea,** then the storm will **stop.**" The **sailors** threw **Jonah** overboard, and the **sea** grew **calm.**

God FORGIVES

As **Jonah** **sank** beneath the waves, a **big fish** swam by and swallowed him up.

Inside the fish **Jonah** **prayed,** "Please help me, **God!**" **God listened.** He told the fish to spit **Jonah** out on the **beach.**

108

Scan to listen.

So **Jonah** went to Nineveh. The **people** listened to him. They **promised** to **stop** being wicked.

"I forgive them," **God** told **Jonah.** But **Jonah** was angry. He did not want **God** to forgive his **enemies.**

Jonah 1–4

109

A LOST BOOK is found

God's temple in **Jerusalem** was **falling apart,** so **King Josiah** sent **builders** and **decorators** to **mend** it.

There they **found** the lost copy of **God's Law.** A **servant** read it to **King Josiah.** He **burst into tears.**

Scan to listen.

"We **haven't obeyed** God!" he cried.

God sent **Josiah** a **message:** "There will be **trouble** later but not for you, **Josiah**. I **know** you **love** me!"

2 Chronicles 34

111

JEREMIAH is rescued

After **good** King Josiah, there were mo[r]e **bad kings. God's** messenger **Jeremiah** warned them that their **enemies** would **fight** them and **win** if they kept **disobeying** God.

The **leaders** got **angry.** They **threw** **Jeremiah** into a deep, muddy **hole.**

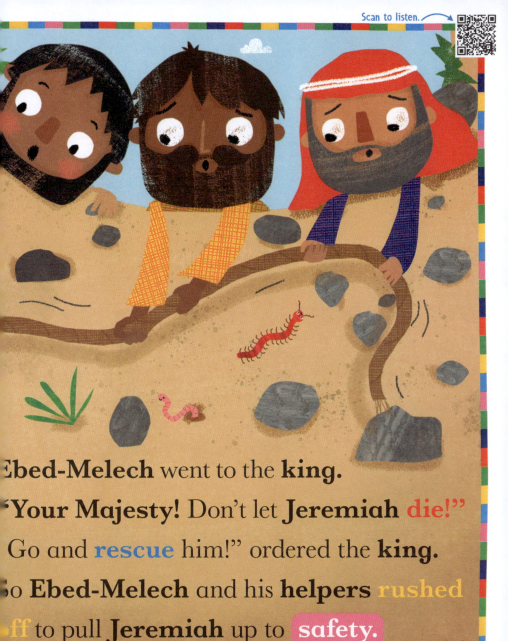

Ebed-Melech went to the **king.**

"Your Majesty! Don't let **Jeremiah** die!"

"Go and rescue him!" ordered the **king.**

So **Ebed-Melech** and his **helpers** rushed

off to pull **Jeremiah** up to safety.

Jeremiah 38

113

Leaving JERUSALEM

No one listened to **Jeremiah's** message from **God.**

Then **Nebuchadnezzar,** mighty king of Babylonia, brought his **army** to attack Jerusalem.

They stole the temple treasure and marched the **people** off to **Babylonia.**

"**Burn** the **city**!" Nebuchadnezzar ordered. How **sad** **God's** people were as they left the **city** and the **land** **God** had **given** them!

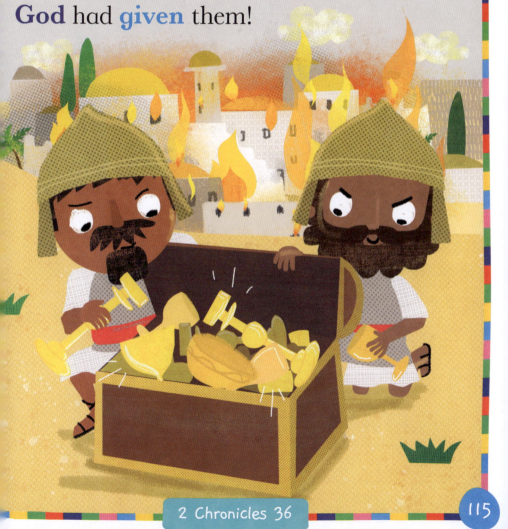

2 Chronicles 36

DANIEL

Israel's **smartest** young **men** were taken to **Nebuchadnezzar's palace.**

"Eat the food the **king** sends you," the **chief servant** ordered.

But **Daniel, Shadrach, Meshach,** and **Abednego** knew that meant **obeying the king** rather than **God.**

Scan to listen.

"Give us **vegetables** and **water** for ten days," **Daniel** begged. The **servant** agreed.

After ten days they looked **fit and healthy.** "These **men** are the **best!**" **Nebuchadnezzar** said. "They will help me rule."

Daniel 1

117

SAVED from the FIRE

"**Bow down**" to my **wonderful gold statue!**" **Nebuchadnezzar** ordered. **Everyone** bowed down except **Shadrach, Meshach,** and **Abednego**

"**Bow down!**" **Nebuchadnezzar** shouted. "Or I'll **throw** you into the **fire!**"

118

Scan to listen.

"We bow only to **God!**" the **friends** replied **bravely.** So **Nebuchadnezzar's soldiers threw** them into the flames.

Suddenly **Nebuchadnezzar gasped:** "We **threw** three **men** in, but there are **four walking about** in the fire! Their **God** has sent his **angel** to **keep** them **safe!**"

Daniel 3

119

DANIEL and the LIONS

The new **king** liked **Daniel.** This made **people** jealous. "Order **everyone** to pray to you alone or be **thrown** to the lions," they told the **king.**

"**Daniel** is still praying to God!" said his **enemies.** So the **king's soldiers** threw **Daniel** into the lions' pit.

The **king** lay awake **worrying.**
The next morning he shouted, **"Daniel!**
Did **God** save you?"
"Yes!" **Daniel** replied.
"My **God** closed the lions'
mouths! I'm safe."

Daniel 6

QUEEN ESTHER

"I **want** a queen," said the **king** of Pers

"Bring me the most **beautiful girls**

in the **kingdom**."

The **king chose** Esther. But he did

not know that **Esther** and her

cousin **Mordecai** were **Jews**.

Haman **hated** **Mordecai,** so he said to the **king,** "Let's **kill** those **Jews** from Israel." The king **agreed.**

Mordecai sent **Esther** a secret message: "Help us!" he **begged.** "**God** made you **queen** to **save** your **people.**"

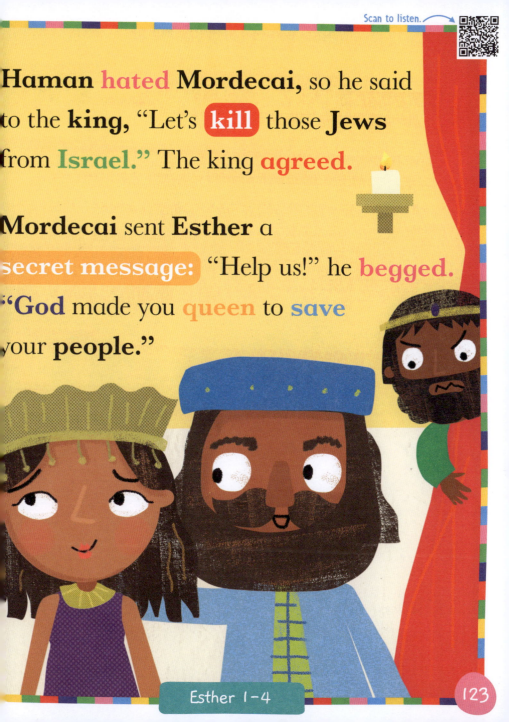

Esther 1–4

123

ESTHER saves the JEWS

"I will **help**," **Esther** told **Mordecai**. "**Pray** that the **king** will not be **angry!**"

Then, **trembling,** she went to the **kin**
He **welcomed** he

"Please come to **dinner,** and bring **Haman,** your **chief adviser,**" **Esther** said.

After dinner **Esther** said, "Your Majesty, an **enemy** wants to **kill** me and my **people!**"

"Who is he?" the **king** asked.

Esther pointed to **Haman.**

"Take him **away!**" the **king** ordered.

"**Mordecai** will **take his place.**"

Esther 5, 7

Rebuilding JERUSALEM

After many years the **Jewish people** came **home,** just as **God** had **promise**

Jerusalem was in **ruins.** So the **people** began **rebuilding** the **temple.**

Scan to listen.

Ezra the **priest** helped them **finish** it and **taught** them **God's Word.**

"Now let's **rebuild** the **city wall,**" said **Nehemiah. "God** will **help** us!" So the **people** worked together, each **family** mending a part of the **wall.**

Ezra 3; Nehemiah 2, 3, 8

127

Give THANKS to GOD

At last the wall was **finished!**
Nehemiah called **everyone** to **celebrat**

Two groups of **singers** and **musicians** marched around Jerusalem. The **people** sang, played their instruments, danced, and thanked G

They all met up at the **temple.**
Everyone was happy because **God**
had **kept** his promise. The **people**
of Israel had come home!

Nehemiah 6, 12

129

NEW TESTAMENT Stories

An ANGEL visits MARY

One day **God** **sent** the angel **Gabriel** to see **Mary. "Mary,** don't be **afraid, God** is **pleased** with you," **Gabriel** said "You are going to have a baby. **Call** him **Jesus.** He will be a **great king**

Mary looked **puzzled.**
"The **baby** will be God's Son,"
Gabriel explained.

"I will do whatever **God** wants,"
Mary replied.

Luke 1

133

MARY visits ELIZABETH

Mary couldn't wait to **tell** her cousin **Elizabeth** the news. She left **home** and hurried off. **"Elizabeth!"** she called, running to the **house.**

Elizabeth hugged her. **"Mary!** How wonderful! As soon as I heard you, I knew that **God** had chosen you to be the **mother** of his **promised king!"**

Scan to listen.

Mary was so **happy** she sang "thank you" to **God.**

Luke 1

135

A special MESSAGE

Joseph wanted to marry **Mary.** When he heard about **Mary's baby,** he was worried. That night **God's angel** gave **Joseph** a special message.

"**Joseph,** don't worry!" the **angel** said. "**God wants** you to marry **Mary.** Her **baby** has been made by **God's** Holy Spirit. Call him **Jesus.** One day he will rescue **God's people.**"

So **Joseph married Mary.**

JESUS is BORN

Bethlehem was **busy**. **Mary** and **Joseph** had come all the way from **Nazareth**. They needed **somewhere** to sleep, but all the **inns** were **full**.

At last **Joseph** found somewhere warm and dry – a **stable!**

That night **Jesus** was born. **Mary** wrapped him up **warmly** and laid him to sleep in the hay.

The SHEPHERDS

Shepherds were looking after their sheep when an **angel** appeared. God's dazzling light shone around.

"Don't be afraid!" said the **angel.** "I have good news! God's special ki has been born in Bethlehem. You will find him lying in a manger."

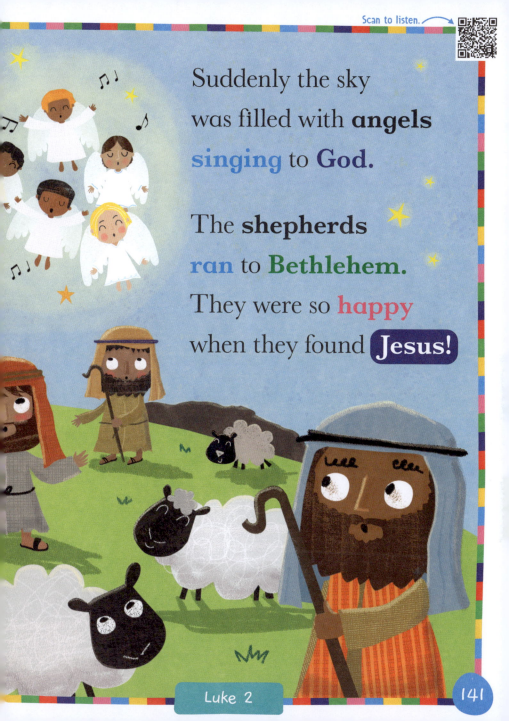

Suddenly the sky was filled with **angels** singing to **God.**

The **shepherds** ran to **Bethlehem.** They were so **happy** when they found **Jesus!**

Luke 2

A PROMISE fulfilled

One day **Mary** and **Joseph** took baby **Jesus** to the temple. There they met an old man called **Simeon**.

Scan to listen.

Simeon had loved **God** all his life. He took **Jesus** gently in his arms. "I'm so happy today!" he said. "Thank you, **God,** for keeping your promise and letting me see the **king** who will rescue us all."

Luke 2

143

The WISE MEN

Far away in the **East,** some **wise men** saw a bright new star.

"How **wonderful!**" they cried.
"A **great king** has been **born.**
Let's go and **worship** him!"
So they followed the star until it stopped over a house in **Bethlehem.**

The **wise men** were so happy to see **Jesus.** They bowed down low and gave him precious gifts of gold, frankincense, and myrrh.

Matthew 2

145

LEAVING for EGYPT

After the **wise men** had gone, **Joseph** saw an **angel** in his dreams.

"Joseph! Get up!" said the **angel.** "Hurry! **Cruel King Herod** wants to **hurt** Jesus. Go to **Egypt.** You will all be **safe** there. I will tell you when to **come back."**

Scan to listen.

Joseph leapt out of bed. He **woke** **Mary** and **Jesus.** They packed their bags and **left** at once.

After **King Herod** died, an **angel** **told** **Joseph** it was **safe** to return **home.**

Matthew 2

147

JESUS in the TEMPLE

Mary, Joseph, and **Jesus** had been **worshipping God** in Jerusalem. They were returning home to **Nazareth.**

"Have you seen **Jesus?**" **Mary** asked. **Joseph** shook his head. Oh no! **Jesus** had been left behind.

Mary and **Joseph** rushed back to **Jerusalem.** They **found Jesus** in the **temple.** "I've been here in my **Father's** **house,**" said **Jesus.**

Luke 2

JOHN baptizes JESUS

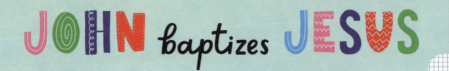

"**Come back** to **God!**" **John** shouted. "Say you are **sorry** and get **baptized** in the water so that **God** will **forgive** you and make you **clean** inside and out!"

The **people** did what **John** told them.

Jesus was good. But he came to be baptized too. He always did what God wanted.

When Jesus came out of the water, God said, "You are my own dear Son. I am pleased with you!"

Mark 1

151

A TEST for JESUS

Jesus went into the desert to **get ready** to do **God's** work. **God's enemy,** the **devil,** came to trick **Jesus.**

"I'll give you the whole **world,** if you **bow down to me,"** he said.

"No!" said **Jesus. "God** has told **everyone** to bow down and **serve** no one else but him."

Jesus chose to listen to **God,** not the **devil,** so the **devil** left.

Matthew 4

ANDREW meets JESUS

One day **Andrew** and his **friend** **followed** Jesus. "Where do you live?" **Andrew** called out. "Come and see!" said **Jesus.**

Scan to listen.

So they went to **Jesus' house** and **talked** with him all afternoon.

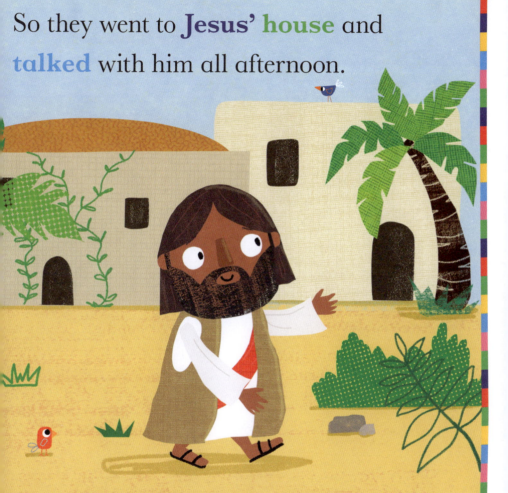

Then **Andrew** rushed to find his brother. "Peter!" he said. "Come and **meet Jesus**; he's the **king God promised** us!"

John 1

155

PETER goes FISHING

Jesus was at the lake telling people about God. He climbed into Peter's boat. "Let's go fishing!" he said.

"I've been fishing. I didn't catch anything!" Peter replied. But he did what Jesus said.

Suddenly the nets were bursting with wriggling fish. Peter was amazed.

"**Peter,** come with me and we'll go **fishing** for people!" **Jesus** said. So **Peter** left his boat and followed **Jesus.**

WATER into WINE

Mary and **Jesus** were at a wedding. **Mary** was worried. **"Jesus,** there's no more wine!"

"Fill these big jars with water," **Jesus** told the **servants.** "Then give some to the **man** in charge."

When the **servants** did what **Jesus** told them, they were amazed. **Jesus** had turned ordinary water into the very best wine!

159

WALKING *again*

"**Jesus** will **help** you **walk** again," said the **men** as they **carried** their **friend** to **Jesus' house.**

The **house** was too **crowded.** So they **dug** a hole in the **roof** and lowered their **friend** down.

Jesus **smiled** and said to the **man,**
"I forgive you. Now **get up**
and walk **home!"**
To **everyone's** amazement the **man**
stood up and began to **walk!**

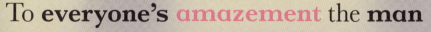

Mark 2

161

A WISE man and a FOOLISH man

One day **Jesus** told a story:

There was once a **foolish** **man** who **built** his **house** on the **sand.** But the **wise** **man** **built** his **house** on the **rock**

Scan to listen.

The wind shook the **houses.** The rain **poured** down; the **floods** rose. The **house** on the sand fell … **CRASH!** But the **wise man** was **safe.**

"If you do what I **tell** you," said **Jesus,** "you will be **safe** too!"

Matthew 7

163

The TRUSTING soldier

An **important soldier** came to see **Jesus.** "My **servant** is very **sick!**" he said.

"I'll **come** and make him **well,**" said **Jesus.**

"You **don't need** to come to my **house,**" the **soldier** said. "Just **give** the order and my **servant** will **get better.**"

"I'm **pleased** you **trust** me so much!" said **Jesus.** "Go **home;** your **servant** is **well** now."

Buried TREASURE

"When you **find God's** kingdom, you will never let it go," **Jesus** said to his **friends.** And he told them this **story:**

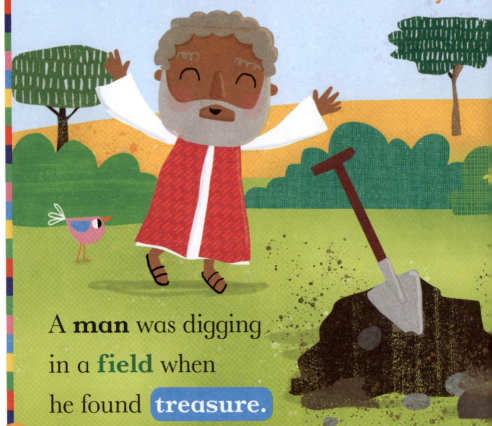

A **man** was digging in a **field** when he found treasure.

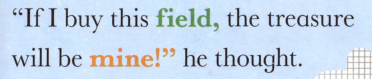

"If I buy this **field,** the treasure will be **mine!**" he thought.

So he **sold** everything he had. Then he **bought** the **field.** He was so **happy!** Now the **treasure** was his forever!

Matthew 13

The STORY of the SEEDS

"If you **listen** to me," said **Jesus,** "you'll be like the **good soil** in this **story**

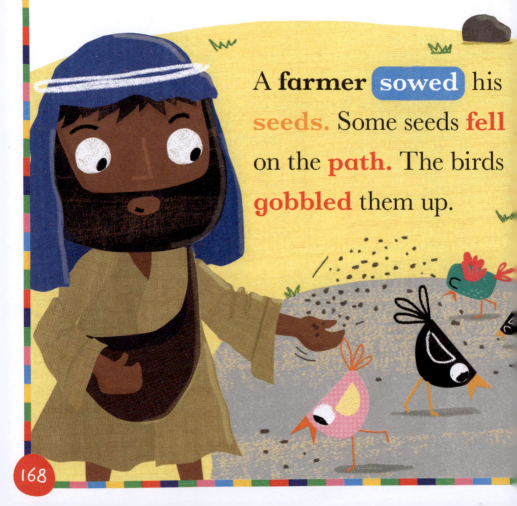

A **farmer** sowed his **seeds.** Some seeds **fell** on the **path.** The birds **gobbled** them up.

The seeds among the **stones** grew quickly, but they **dried up** in the **hot sun.**

Other seeds grew well until the **weeds** got in their way.

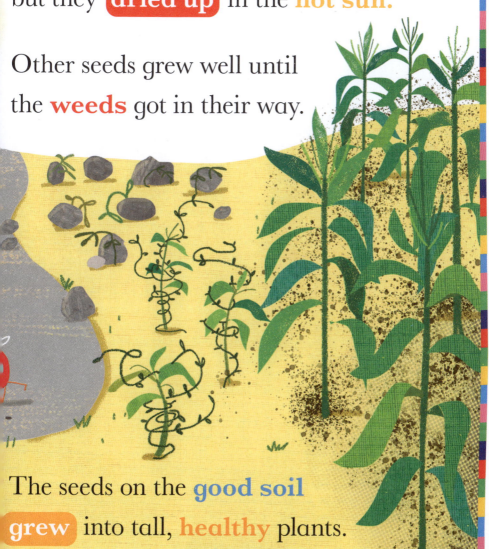

The seeds on the **good soil** **grew** into tall, **healthy** plants.

Mark 4

169

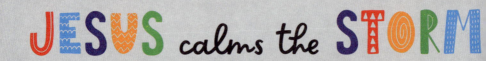

JESUS calms the STORM

It had been a **busy** day. **Jesus** was fast asleep in his **friends' boat.**

Suddenly a wild wind whipped up the waves. They came **crashing** over the **boat.**

"**Wake up, Jesus!**" his **friends** shouted.

"The **boat** is **sinking!**"

Jesus got up. "Waves! Calm down!"

He ordered, "Wind, be **quiet!**"

At once all was **safe** and **still**. **Jesus'**
friends were amazed. "Even the
wind and waves do what **Jesus** says!"

Mark 4

171

The SICK GIRL

Jairus' daughter was very sick. "Jesus please make her **better!**" he **begged.**

Just then his **servant** ran up. "Your **daughter** is **dead,**" he said **sadly.** "Trust me, **Jairus,**" **Jesus** said **gently,** "your little **girl** will **get well.**"

At **Jairus' house everyone** was crying. The **girl** was lying pale and still.

"Little **girl,**" **Jesus** said, taking her hand, "**get up!**" She **opened** her eyes and stood up. She was alive and **well.**

JESUS and the BLIND MEN

As **Jesus** left **Jairus' house,** two **blind men** shouted out, **"Jesus,** be kind and **help** us!"

"Do you **believe** I can make you **better?"** **Jesus** asked. "Oh yes!" they replied.

"Then because you **believe** in me, it will **happen,"** said **Jesus** as he reached out and **touched** their eyes.

At once the **men** could **see!**

Matthew 9

175

FOOD for EVERYONE

The **crowd** had **listened** to **Jesus** all day.

"They're **hungry**," said **Jesus**. "Let's **give** them some food."

"We **don't** have enough money!" his **friends** replied.

"This **boy** has five little **loaves** and two **fish**," said **Andrew.**

Jesus **took** the loaves and the fish and **thanked** **God** for them. Then he **handed out** the food. And **everyone** had **plenty** to eat!

JESUS walks on WATER

One evening **Jesus** went **away** to **pray.**
His **friends** **set off** across the  lake.
They puffed and panted as they rowed.

Suddenly they saw **someone** walking on the **water** toward them.
"It's a **ghost!**" they screamed.

"Don't be scared," said the **man**, climbing into their boat. "It's me, Jesus!"
The **friends** were amazed. It was Jesus!

Mark 6

179

GOD talks to JESUS

Jesus took **Peter, James,** and **John** up a **mountain** to pray.

Jesus grew **brighter** and **brighter** until even his clothes **shone** **dazzling white** The **friends** were **amazed.**

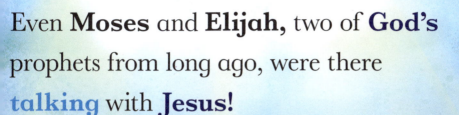

Even **Moses** and **Elijah,** two of **God's** prophets from long ago, were there **talking** with **Jesus!**

Suddenly a **misty cloud** came down and they heard **God** say, "This is my **Son. Listen** to him!"

The KIND STRANGER

Jesus told another **story:**
A **man** was lying badly **hurt** by the side
of the **road.**

A **priest** came along.
But he **did not help;**
he just walked away!

Then another **important man** walked b
But he **did not stop** to help either.

Scan to listen.

At last, a **kind** **stranger** **stopped.**
He **bandaged** the **man,** **took** him
to an **inn,** and looked after him there.
"Be kind like that **stranger** in the story,"
said **Jesus.**

MARTHA and MARY

Jesus was at **Martha** and **Mary's** house.
Mary sat down to listen to **Jesus.**
But **Martha** rushed around getting the
food ready.

Martha was **upset.** **"Jesus!"** she said. "I'm doing **all** the work by **myself.** Tell **Mary** to help me!"

"Oh, **Martha,"** said **Jesus** gently, **"Mary** wants to be with me. She has chosen what is most **important."**

Luke 10

A PRAYER to GOD

"**Jesus,** teach us how to **talk** to **God,**" his **friends** asked. So **Jesus taught** them this **prayer:**

Our **Father** in heaven,
may **everyone know** and **love** you.
Come and be our **King.**
Give us today the food we **need.**
Forgive the **bad things** we do.
Help us to forgive others too.
When we want to do something **bad,**
help us **choose** to do **good** instead.

Luke 11

Saying THANK YOU

One day **Jesus** met some **men** with a **skin disease.** "**Jesus,** please make us **better!**" they called.

"**Find** the **priest,**" **Jesus** said kindly, "so he can see you are well again."

As the **men** set off, they **saw** that their skin was as **good as new!**

But only **one** of them rushed back to **thank** **Jesus.**

Luke 17

189

The PARTY

"God invites people into his **kingdom**," **Jesus** said, "like the **man** who was getting ready for his **party**.

"The **important people** he had **invited** sent **messages** saying, 'We're sorry, we're **too busy** to come.'

"Then the **man** told his **servants,** '**Go!** Find the **people** who are **never invited** to parties and **bring** them **here.**' Soon the **man's house** was full of **people** having **fun.**"

The LOST SHEEP

Everyone crowded around as **Jesus** told this **story** about what **God's** kingdom is like:

There was once a **shepherd** who had **one hundred sheep.** One day he discovered one was **missing.**

He **searched** up and down, near and far.
Finally he **found** it. He was so **happy** he
carried it all the way **home!**

"I've **found** my **lost sheep!**"
he called to his **friends.**
"Let's have a **party!**"
Like the **shepherd** in the story,
God is **happy** when even one
sinner **turns back** to him.

Luke 15

193

Coming HOME

There was once a **son** who **left** home.
He soon **spent** his **father's** money.

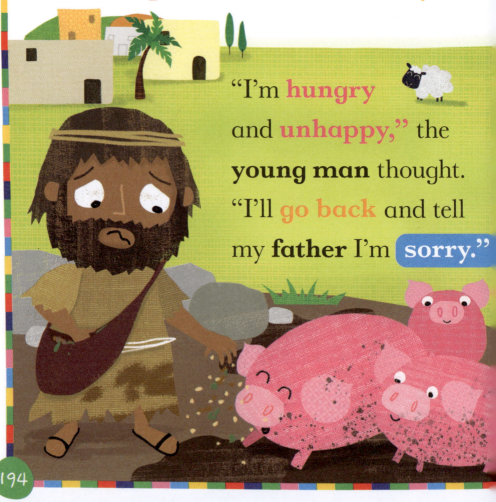

"I'm **hungry** and **unhappy**," the **young man** thought. "I'll **go back** and tell my **father** I'm sorry."

As soon as his **father** saw him, he ran to **hug** him. "My **son** has come **home!**" he called to his **servants.** "Let's have a **party!**"

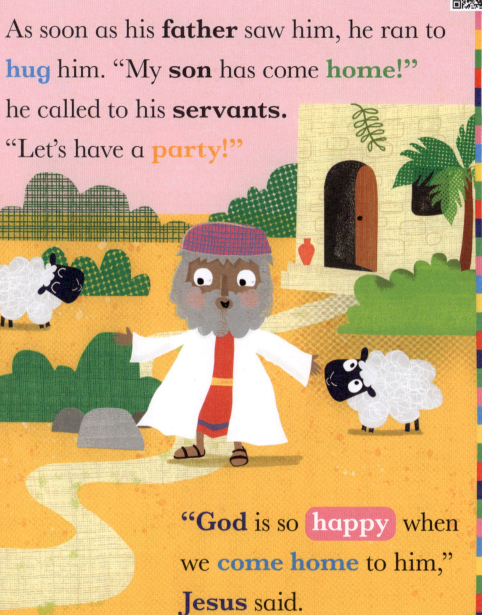

"**God** is so happy when we **come home** to him," **Jesus** said.

Please FORGIVE me!

Two **men** went to the temple to **pray.** The first **man** said, **"God,** I keep all your rules; I don't cheat or steal like that **man** there."

The second **man** stood sadly at the back. "I know I'm a bad man, **God.**" He prayed, "Please forgive me."

"**Guess** which **man God** was pleased with," said **Jesus.** "The one who said he was sorry."

Luke 18

JESUS gives new LIFE

Martha and **Mary** were very **sad** because their brother **Lazarus** had **died**

"I can **give new life**," **Jesus** said to them. "Anyone who **trusts** me will never really die."

Scan to listen.

He went to the **place** where **Lazarus** was buried. "Move the stone away!" **Jesus** ordered. **"Lazarus, come out!"** he called.

nd to **everyone's** amazement, azarus **walked** out alive and well.

John 11

199

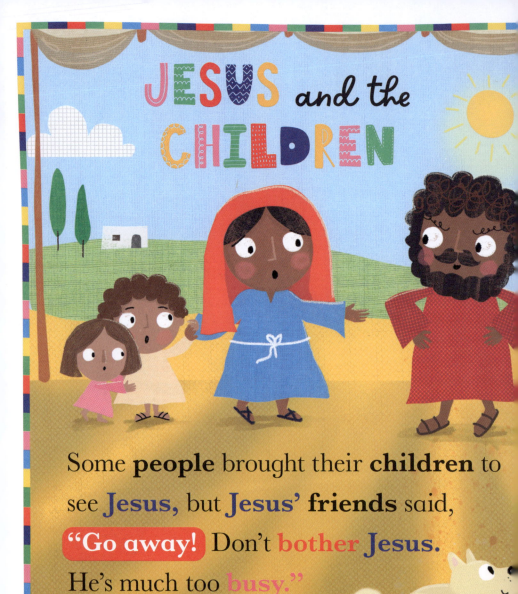

JESUS and the CHILDREN

Some **people** brought their **children** to see **Jesus,** but **Jesus' friends** said, **"Go away!** Don't **bother Jesus.** He's much too **busy."**

Jesus was **upset** with them.

Scan to listen.

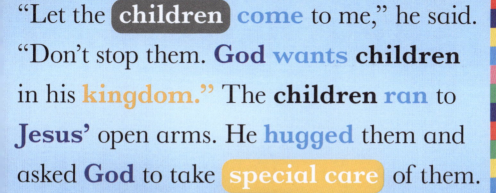

"Let the **children** come to me," he said.
"Don't stop them. **God wants children**
in his **kingdom."** The **children ran** to
Jesus' open arms. He **hugged** them and
asked **God** to take **special care** of them.

Mark 10

201

ZACCHAEUS changes

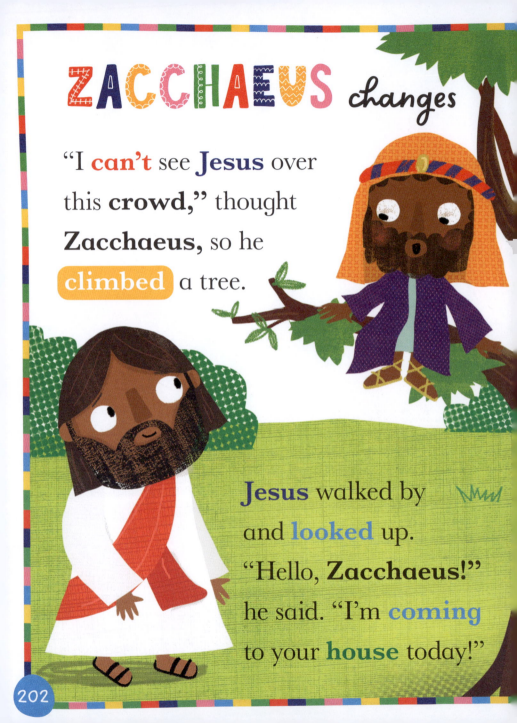

"I **can't** see **Jesus** over this **crowd**," thought **Zacchaeus**, so he **climbed** a tree.

Jesus walked by and **looked** up. "Hello, **Zacchaeus!**" he said. "I'm **coming** to your **house** today!"

202

Scan to listen.

The **crowd** gasped.
Zacchaeus was a cheat; nobody liked him!

Zacchaeus gasped.
Could **Jesus** really **want** to be his **friend?**

Zacchaeus had a **wonderful** day with **Jesus**. And he promised not to cheat anyone again.

Luke 19

203

Expensive PERFUME

As **Jesus** and his **friends** were eating, **Mary** poured her precious bottle of perfume over **Jesus'** feet. Then she wiped them gently with her long hair.

The wonderful, sweet smell filled the room.

"**Mary** should have sold that perfume and given the money to the **poor**," complained **Judas**.

But **Jesus** was pleased with **Mary**. "**Mary** has done something very special for me!" he said.

Entering JERUSALEM

Jesus rode into **Jerusalem** on a young **donkey.** The **people** spread branches and cloaks on the **ground,** like a **carpet** for a king.

The **crowds** waved branches to **welcome** Jesus. **"Hooray** for **God's** special **king!"** they **cheered.**

"Who is this **man?"** **people** asked. "It's **Jesus! God's messenger!"** the **crowds** replied.

Being READY

"Be ready for God's kingdom," said Jesus, as he told this story: There were ten **bridesmaids** who were waiting for the **bridegroom** to arrive.

The wise girls took extra oil for their lamps.

The **foolish** **girls** did not. At midnight their lamps ran out of oil, so they went off to buy more.

Suddenly the **bridegroom** arrived. He took the wise **bridesmaids** to his wedding party. But the foolish **bridesmaids** missed out.

JESUS is ANGRY

God's temple was busy when
Jesus arrived.
"Buy a lamb here,"
shouted some sellers.
"Doves for sale!"
yelled others.

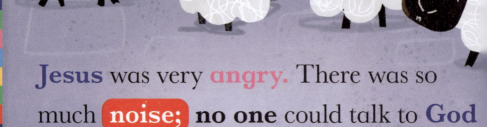

Jesus was very angry. There was so
much noise; no one could talk to God

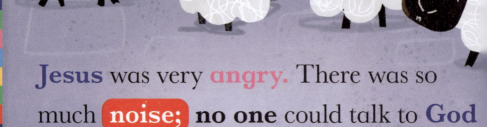

210

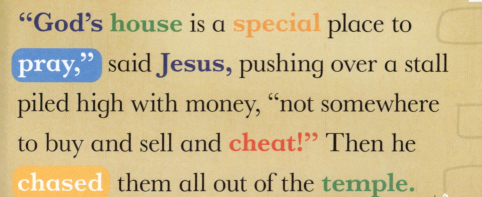

"**God's house** is a **special** place to **pray,**" said **Jesus,** pushing over a stall piled high with money, "not somewhere to buy and sell and **cheat!**" Then he **chased** them all out of the **temple.**

Mark 11

WASHING feet

One evening, during supper, **Jesus** got up, tied a towel around his waist, and began to wash his **friends' feet.**

They were shocked. It was the **servant's** job to wash feet. "**Jesus,** you **mustn't** wash our feet!" said **Peter.**

"I'm washing your feet because I love you," said **Jesus.** "Now copy me. Love and help one another."

A SPECIAL meal

Jesus was eating a **special meal** with his **friends** when he took some **bread, thanked God, broke** it in pieces, and handed it around.

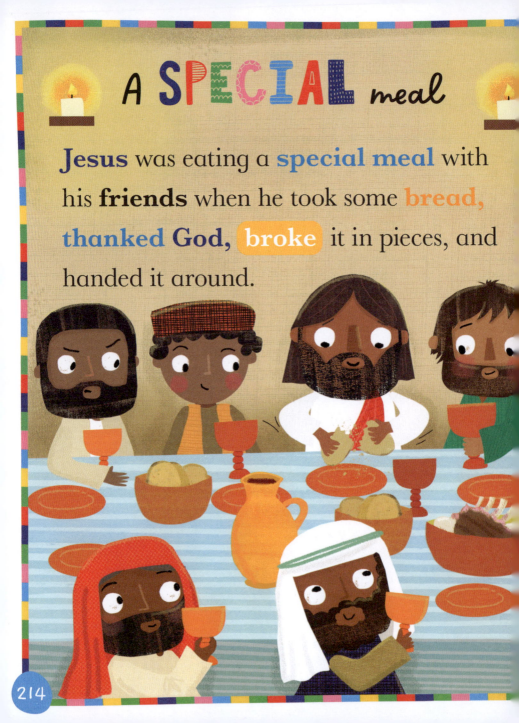

"This is my **body**," he said. "I give it for you." Then he took a **cup of wine, thanked God,** and passed it around. "Drink this," he said. "I will **die for** many people because God has **promised** to **forgive** them."

Matthew 26

215

JESUS is taken PRISONER

Jesus was praying in the garden.
He was sad because he knew he was
going to die soon.

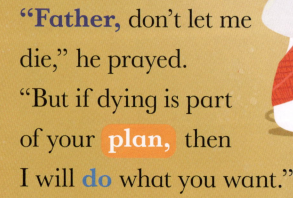

"Father, don't let me
die," he prayed.
"But if dying is part
of your plan, then
I will do what you want."

Scan to listen.

Suddenly **Jesus'** friend **Judas** arrived, **leading** a crowd of **Jesus' enemies!**

He **kissed Jesus.**

At once the **soldiers** surrounded **Jesus** and took him **prisoner.**

Luke 22

PETER lets JESUS down

Peter followed **Jesus** and the **soldiers.** "Aren't you **Jesus'** friend?" asked a **servant girl.**

Peter **shook** his head. **"No!** I don't know him."

Two more **people asked** if he knew **Jesus. "No!"** said **Peter. "No!"**

Suddenly a rooster **crowed. Peter** remembered that **Jesus** had said: "Before the rooster crows, you will say **three times** that you're not my friend." Peter **burst into tears.**

JESUS is left to DIE

Jesus' **enemies** took Jesus to Pilate, the Roman ruler. **Pilate** asked Jesus lots questions. Then he said, "Jesus has not done anything wrong. I will let him go."

"NO!" the **people** shouted. "Kill Jesus! Nail him to a cross!"

Scan to listen.

So **Pilate's soldiers** nailed **Jesus** to a **cross** and **left him to die.**

Jesus knew that he had **done** what **God** **wanted.** "My work is **finished!**" he **cried.** Then he died.

John 18–19

221

A SAD day

Jesus was **dead**. **Nicodemus** and **Jose[p]** of **Arimathea** had been **afraid** to say they were **Jesus'** friends.

But now they **showed** that they **loved** him. They wrapped **Jesus'** body in cloth[s] with **precious perfumes** and **carefull[y]** put him in a new **tomb**.

Together they **rolled** the heavy stone across the doorway. Then they walked **sadly** away.

John 19

223

JESUS is ALIVE!

Two days later, **Mary Magdalene** stood outside **Jesus' tomb.** It was empty! **Jesus'** body was gone!

"Why are you crying?" asked a **man** standing nearby.

"Have you taken **Jesus** away?" **Mary sobbed.**

"Mary!" said the **man gently. Mary** looked up. It was **Jesus!** He smiled. "Go and tell my **friends."**

Mary ran all the way. She couldn't wait to tell them the good news! **Jesus** was ALIVE!

A SURPRISE

Two of **Jesus'** **friends** met a **man** on their way **home.**
"**Jesus** was killed three days ago," they told him, "but **Mary** says **Jesus** is alive again!"

"**God** promised this would happen to his **special king**," said the **stranger**.

At **supper** time, the **man thanked God** for the bread, then **gave** it to the **friends.** Suddenly the **friends** knew that the **stranger** was **Jesus.** He really was **alive!**

Tell EVERYONE!

The two **friends** ran back to **Jerusalem**.
"We've seen **Jesus!**" they said
to all of **Jesus' friends.**

Suddenly **Jesus** was **there** too!
Everyone stopped talking.
"Don't be scared," **Jesus** said.
"It's me. Touch me. I'm not a ghost!"

Scan to listen.

They were so **happy** to see **Jesus** **alive** again.

"Tell everyone **everywhere** about me," **Jesus** told them. "Because of me, they can be **God's friends** again."

THOMAS believes

Thomas didn't believe Jesus was **alive.** "When I have **seen** and **touched Jesus** for myself, then I'll believe," he said.

Scan to listen.

A week later, **Jesus** came again.
"**Thomas,** look! Touch my hands and
feet. It really is me," **Jesus** said.
Thomas gazed at him.
"My **Lord** and my **God!**" he said.

"Now you believe!" said **Jesus.**
"**God** is pleased with **people** who
believe even if they don't see me."

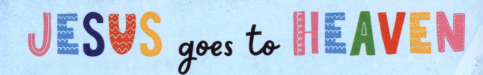

JESUS goes to HEAVEN

"Wait in **Jerusalem**," **Jesus** told his friends. "**God** will **send** you his **Holy Spirit.** He will **help** you **tell** the **whole world** about me."

Then, before their eyes, **Jesus** was **taken up** to **heaven**. Suddenly two **men** dressed in white appeared.

"Why are you standing **here** looking at the **sky?**" they asked. **"Jesus** will **come back** one day."

Acts 1

The HOLY SPIRIT

Jesus' **friends** were **praying** when…
Whoosh! A sound like a **rushing wind**
roared through the **house.**

A **flickering flame** rested **gently** on
each head. **God's** **Holy Spirit** had come
to **help** them **tell others** about **Jesus.**

When the **people** from other countries heard what **God** had done, they **wanted** to be **Jesus' friends** too.

Acts 2

235

A man WALKS again

Peter and **John** were going to the **temple.**

"Please give me money!" begged a **man** who **could not walk.**
"I don't have any," **Peter** said kindly,
"but I **know** Jesus, God's Son.
And **Jesus** tells you to walk!"

Right away the **man's** feet and legs were **strong** again. He could **walk, run,** and **jump!** "**Thank you!**" he shouted. "**God** is **great!**"

Acts 3

An IMPORTANT man

God's **angel** sent **Philip** to a dusty **desert road.** The chariot of an **important African man** rumbled by.

"Keep up with that chariot, **Philip,**" said **God's Holy Spirit. Philip** ran alongside. He heard the **man** reading **God's book.** "Do you understand it?" asked **Philip.**

"No," **sighed** the **man.**
"What does it mean?"

Philip explained that
it was all about **Jesus,**
and the **man** decided to
become **Jesus' friend** too.

Acts 8

239

JESUS speaks to PAUL

Paul did **not believe** that **Jesus** was **God's** special **king.** He hated **Jesus'** **friends.** He set off to find them and put them in **prison.**

FLASH! A bright light shone. **Paul** fell to the **ground.** "**Paul,** why do you hate me and **hurt** me?" said a **voice.**

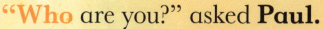

"**Who** are you?" asked **Paul.**

"I am **Jesus!**"

Paul was shocked.

Jesus was alive!

From that moment **Paul**

became **Jesus' friend.**

"**Go** and **tell everyone**

about me," **Jesus** said.

Acts 9

241

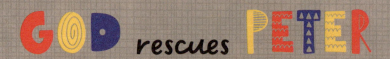

GOD rescues PETER

Peter was in **prison.** The **soldiers** guarded him night and day.
One night an **angel** shook **Peter** awake.
Peter's chains fell to the ground.

242

"Quick, put on your sandals," said the **angel.** "Follow me."

So **Peter** followed the **angel** past the **guards,** through the gate, and into the street. Then the **angel** disappeared. **Peter** blinked. It wasn't a dream. He really was free!

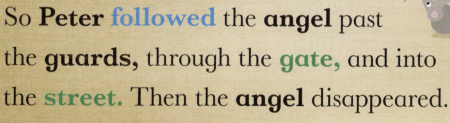

Acts 12

FRIENDS of JESUS

Paul **journeyed** to many **places** **telling** people about **Jesus.**

One night a **man** called to **Paul** in a **dream,** "Come to **Macedonia!** **Help us!**" The next day **Paul** sailed to **Macedonia.**

There he **met** **Lydia,** a rich woman, and her **friends.** He told them about **Jesus.** So **Lydia** and her **friends** became **friends** of **Jesus** too.

Acts 16

PAUL is taken PRISONER

One day when **Paul** was at the **temple,** **Jesus' enemies** tried to **kill** him. "**Paul tells lies!**" they shouted.

Just then the **Roman commander** marched in. His **soldiers** stopped the **people** from hurting **Paul.**

Paul explained that **God** wanted **everyone** to know **Jesus** was alive, but the **crowd** shouted, "NO! Get rid of **Paul.**" So the **commander** put **Paul** in prison.

Acts 21, 22

247

GOD keeps his PROMISE

"The **Roman emperor** must decide if I am right," **Paul** said.

So the **soldiers** took **Paul** and set sail for Rome. Before long, the ship was **caught** in a raging storm.

"Don't be afraid," said **Paul.** "**God** will keep us all safe."

As the ship broke up, **everyone** swam for the **shore.** At last they reached the land, cold and wet, but safe. **God** had kept his promise.

LETTERS from PAUL

Finally **Paul** and the **soldiers** arrived in **Rome.**

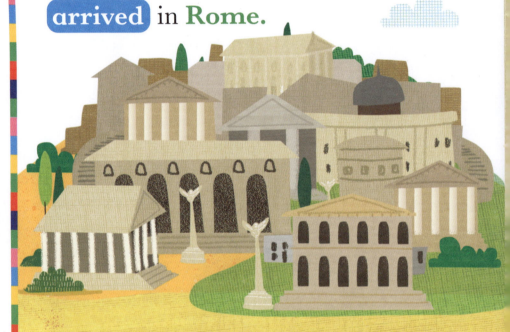

Paul was still a prisoner, but he was allowed to write to all the **people** he had met on his travels. They had become **friends** of **Jesus** too.

They told **Paul** their **problems** and he **wrote back** to **help** them.

"Keep on **loving Jesus**," **Paul** wrote, "and keep on **loving each other**."

Acts 28

251

A NEW HEAVEN and EARTH

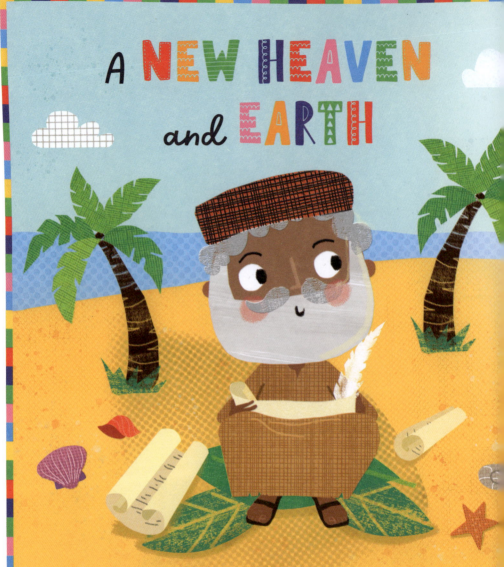

One day **John** saw a **man**. He was **stron**
good, and **shining bright**. It was **Jesu**

"**Write** to my **friends**,"
Jesus said. "**Tell** them that
God is going to **make** a **new**
heaven and a **new earth**
where **no one** will be hurt or die!
All **God's friends** will **live**
with him **forever**."

Revelation 1, 21

253

INDEX

This index shows where to find some well-known Bible stories in this book and also shows groups of stories that link together.

The OLD TESTAMENT

The NEW TESTAMENT

FIRST MENTIONS: Find a Character